LUCE LÓPEZ-BARALT earned her Ph.D. at Harvard University. She is Distinguished Professor and Professor Emerita of Spanish and Comparative Literatures at the University of Puerto Rico. She has been awarded the Guggenheim, Fulbright, Erasmus, National Endowment for the Humanities, and American Council for Learned Societies Fellowships; the Royal Order of Isabel la Católica (awarded by King Philip VI of Spain), the Premio Internacional Henríquez Ureña (México), the Ibn Arabi Prize (Murcia, Spain), the Premio Nacional de las Letras Teresa de Ávila (Spain). She is vicepresident of the Academia Puertorriqueña de la Lengua Española. Her 30 books and more than 300 articles on comparative Spanish and Arabic literatures and mysticism, *aljamiado-moorish* and Latin American literatures have been published in Spanish (*Un kamasutra español*, Vaso Roto Ediciones), English, French, Italian, German, Portuguese, Croatian, Arabic, Dutch, Persian, Chinese, Urdu and Turkish.

ANDREW HURLEY is Professor Emeritus of Translation and English and American Literature, College of Humanities, University of Puerto Rico-Río Piedras. For the last forty years he has also been a translator of Latin American and Peninsular Spanish literature, with more than sixty book-length novels and story collections published by leading U.S. and U.K. publishing houses, in addition to many volumes of academic studies in literary criticism, history, and architecture. Among the dozens of authors he has translated are Jorge Luis Borges (*Collected Fictions* and *The Book of Imaginary Beings*), Ernesto Sabato, Rubén Darío (for Penguin Classics), Reinaldo Arenas (the Pentagony and others), Margo Glantz, Gustavo Saínz, Arturo Pérez-Reverte, Zoé Valdés, Ana Lydia Vega, and Edgardo Rodríguez Juliá. He has also translated uncategorizable "creative [non]fiction" by Antonio Martorell and others, and a number of children's books.

Light Upon Light

First edition: October, 2025
Original Title: Luz sobre Luz

© Luce López-Baralt, 2014
© of the translation: Andrew Hurley, 2025
All rights reserved. Published in the United States of America by Broken Bowl Books

Manufactured in the United States of America
Cover engraving: Víctor Ramírez

Broken Bowl Books
PO BOX 450948
Laredo TX 78045-0023
www.brokenbowlbooks.com

Total or partial reproduction of this work, by any means or process whatsoever, is strictly forbidden without the written authorization of the copyright holders under the sanctions established by the law.

ISBN: 978-1-969317-03-3
Library of Congress Control Number: 2025946976

Luce López Baralt
Light Upon Light

Translated by Andrew Hurley

Broken Bowl / Books

Luz sobre luz:
Dios guía a su Luz a quien Él quiere.

(CORÁN XXIV, 35)

Parécele [al alma] que toda junta ha estado en otra región muy diferente de en esta que vivimos, adonde se le muestra otra luz tan diferente de la de acá, que si toda su vida ella la estuviera fabricando [...] fuera imposible alcanzarla...

(SANTA TERESA DE JESÚS
Moradas VI, 5)

Light upon light.
Allah guides to His light whom He wills.
Qu'ran 24, 35

[The soul] feels that she has been wholly transported into another and a very different region from that in which we live, where a light so unearthly [shines] that, if during her whole lifetime she had been trying to picture it. . ., she could not possibly have succeeded.

St. Teresa of Ávila,
Interior Castle, Dwelling 6, Chapter 5, section 8.1

---

1   *The Interior Castle, or The Mansions*, trans. by the Benedictines of Stanbrook, rev. and ed. by Benedict Zimmerman, Grand Rapids, MI: Christian Classics Ethereal Library, based on a text published in London by Thomas Baker, 1921.

Índice / Contents

16 Prefacio / *Introduction*
26 Palabras preliminares / *Preface*

32 LUZ SOBRE LUZ / *LIGHT UPON LIGHT*
  Quien gusta el vino que yo bebí] 34
  [Those who taste the wine I drank,] 35
  [Aquel día bebí un sorbo de cielo] 36
  [That day I drank a sip of heaven] 37
  [Acerqué a mis labios] 38
  [I brought to my lips] 39
  [Te abracé abisalmente] 40
  [I embraced You abyssally] 41
  [El diamante irisado de mi alma] 42
  [The iridescent diamond of my soul] 43
  [El misterio del Amor] 44
  [The mystery of Love,] 45
  [La inmensa cítara de la noche] 46
  [Night's immense zither] 47
  [Logré escuchar las estrellas sonoras] 48
  [At last I heard the vibrating stars] 49
  [Ay, Amor,] 50
  [Ay, Love,] 51
  [La fragancia del sol,] 52
  [The fragrance of the sun,] 53
  [Plantamos un huerto en las esferas:] 54
  [We planted a garden in the spheres] 55
  [Desaparecen el invocante] 56
  [The invoker and invoked] 57
  [Me vestiste de Ti mismo] 58
  [You clothed me in Yourself] 59
  [Era Tu perla escondida:] 60
  [I was Your hidden pearl.] 61
  [Me diluí en Tu esencia] 62
  [diluted into Your essence] 63
  [A la vera del agua] 64

[At the water's edge,]   65
[Bebí de la fuente]   66
[I drank from the fountain]   67
[Me amaste con tal ímpetu]   68
[You loved me with such vehemence]   69
[¡Soy la luna llena que asciende!]   70
[I am the full moon rising!]   71
[Los horizontes quedaron libres]   72
[The horizons were swept free]   73
[Iba nocturna por las islas umbrías]   74
[I was traveling at night through the shadowy islands]   75
[Entro en la alfaguara plateada.]   76
[I slip into the silvery spring.]   77
[Al hacerme tuya]   78
[When I became yours]   79
[Aspiré a ser Tu espejo]   80
[I aspired to be Your mirror]   81
[Soy un palacio sin tiempo]   82
[I am a palace outside time.]   83
[Colapsan los hexágonos,]   84
[The hexagons, the triangles, and the trefoils]   85
Tú   86
You   87
Luz no usada]   88
[Light so strange]   89
[Y la caballería]   90
[And the cavalry,]   91
[Creía]   92
[I thought]   93
[Recibí]   94
[I received]   95
[bésame]   96
[kiss me]   97
[Qué bien sé yo]   98
[How fully I know]   99
[De súbito]   102
[Suddenly]   103
[Dentro de este mísero cuerpo de arcilla]   104
[Within this meager body of clay]   105
Lo que supe   106

What I Learned   107
Me sumerjo en un mar blanco sin orillas]   108
[I float in a white, shoreless sea]   109
Domine non sum digna   110
Domine non sum digna   111
Salgo a la noche,]   112
[I go out into the night.]   113
[La fuente era un cielo nocturno]   114
[The fountain was a night sky]   115
[Una mirada sola]   116
[A single gaze]   117
[El pájaro del día]   118
[The bird of day]   119
[La Rosa era invisible]   120
[The Rose was invisible]   121
[Salí de Tu mar en calma]   122
[I came out of Your calm sea]   123
[Como la flor de loto]   124
[Like the lotus-flower]   125
[Niels Bohr proclama la pluralidad de los mundos]   126
[Niels Bohr proclaims the multiplicity of worlds]   127
[Cultivo un huerto de estrellas:]   128
[I tend a garden of stars.]   129
[Me engalanaste con luceros]   130
[You bedecked me with bright stars]   131
[Camino sin pasos hacia Ti]   132
[I walk toward You without walking,]   133
[Penetré en la luz blanca]   134
[I penetrated the white light]   135
[Me elevo de sombra en sombra]   136
[I rise from shadow to shadow.]   137
[Mi Rosa inmarcesible,]   138
[My unfading Rose,]   139
[En la ráfaga verde]   140
[In the green gust of wind]   141
[La luz de la luna penetra sigilosa en el estanque]   142
[Stealthily, the light of the moon enters the pool,]   143
Entrando a los castillos interiores   144
Entering the Interior Castles   145
¡Cómo ardía la luz]   146

[How the light blazed]   147
[Eggidio di Assisi confesó:]   148
[Giles of Assisi's confession:]   149
Más allá de Shabistari   150
Beyond Shabistari   151
Los ruiseñores bajo la nieve   152
Nightingales in the Snowfall   153
La montaña liberada   154
The Mountain Freed   155
Segunda Epístola a los Corintios   156
The Second Epistle to the Corinthians   157
Nuestro lecho florido   158
Our Flower-Strewn Bed   159
En torno a la Azora XXIV, 35   160
On Surah 24: 35   161
Intérprete de los deseos   162
Interpreter of Desires   163
Abu l-Hasan al-Sushtari]   164
[Abu l-Hasan al-Sushtari]   165
[Angelus Silesius entonó]   166
[Angelus Silesius intoned]   167
[Águila sideral,]   168
[Astral Eagle,]   169
[Mi alma se anegó]   170
[My soul drowned]   171
[En un instante habitado por albas y espejos]   172
[In an instant inhabited by dawns and mirrors]   173
[Un pájaro cantó Tu nombre:]   174
[El Alpha se disuelve en el Omega]   176
[The Alpha dissolves in the Omega]   177
[Instante al blanco vivo]   178
[A white-hot instant,]   179

180   CANTO SIN PALABRAS / SONG WITHOUT WORDS
¿Cómo entonar en tierra extraña]   182
[How, in a foreign land, can I sing]   183
[Todo me lo diste Tú:]   184
[You told me all —]   185
[¿Cómo me las arreglo]   186
[How can I manage]   187

[Aunque llorara diamantes]   188
[Even if I wept diamonds]   189
[Nunca más habré de creer en las palabras:]   190
[Never more shall I believe in words.]   191
La música callada   192
Hushed Music   193
Mis palabras:]   194
[My words:]   195
[La pluma corría veloz sobre el papel]   196
[The pen flew swiftly across the paper.]   197
[Calendario de piedra,]   198
[Stone calendar,]   199
El círculo de tinta   200
The Circle of Ink   201
El tintorero Hákim de Merv]   202
[Hakim, the masked dyer of Merv,]   203
[¿Cómo decirlo?]   204
[How to describe it?]   205
Soy tu velo   206
I Am Your Veil   207
Aunque trocara mis palabras]   208
[Though my words were transformed]   209
[Si tuviera lenguaje]   210
[If only I had language,]   211
[La fragancia se desprende]   212
[The fragrance breaks away]   213
[Chuang Tzu yearned for conversation]   215
[Fuera de sí,]   216
[Outside himself,]   217
[Han ardido las palabras]   218
[Words have blazed with fire,]   219
[Mi vaso fue la luna llena]   220
[My cup was the full moon]   221
[Imagino versos,]   222
[I imagine verses,]   223
[Me enseñaste]   224
[You taught me]   225
[Las palabras]   226
[Words]   227
La dicha de enmudecer   228

The Joy of Falling Silent   229
Silencio:]   230
[*Silence:*]   231

232   CANCIONES EN LA NOCHE / SONGS IN THE NIGHT
Un pájaro hunde su grito rojo]   234
[*A bird's red cry is drowned*]   235
[Yo, que una vez]   236
[*I who once*]   237
[Mis oscuros minutos vacíos]   238
[*My dark empty minutes*]   239
[Una vez supe]   240
[*Once I learned*]   241
[Devuelta a esta orilla]   242
[*Washed up again on this shore,*]   243
[Yo fui Una contigo:]   244
[*I was One with You.*]   245
[La senda de amatista]   246
[*The amethyst path*]   247
[Yo tuve un ayer de ruiseñores:]   248
[*I had a yesterday of nightingales:*]   249
[La fuente parpadea en la distancia]   250
[*The fountain twinkles in the distance.*]   251
[Donde Tú estabas]   252
[*Where You once were*]   253
[Dondequiera que haya ruinas]   254
[*Where there are ruins,*]   255
[Entré en el jardín interior]   256
[*I entered the interior garden*]   257
¿Recuerdas?   258
Remember?   259
Una vez reflejé el Sol.]   260
[*Once I reflected the Sun.*]   261
El Sol a medianoche   262
The Sun at Midnight   263
Dime si desde el inmortal seguro]   264
[*Tell me whether, in Your fortress of immortality,*]   265
[Un pájaro canta lo que va a venir:]   266
[*A bird sings what is to come —*]   267

269   TRANSLATOR'S NOTE

Light Upon Light

Prefacio

No es casual que esta colección de poemas de la eminente estudiosa puertorriqueña Luce López-Baralt se titule *Luz sobre luz*, ya que refleja su propio nombre lumínico, Luce. El alma de esta destacada hermeneuta, dedicada tanto a la poesía sufí en lengua árabe como a la poesía mística española, fue iluminada desde su temprana edad por la luz de la espiritualidad cristiana y luego por la luz de las enseñanzas esotéricas del sufismo. *Luz sobre luz* es la traducción del versículo coránico *nurun 'ala 'l-nur*, que forma parte del «Verso de la Luz» del capítulo 24 del Corán. El versículo tiene numerosos niveles de interpretación y puede decirse que en cierto sentido se puede aplicar al alma misma de Luce. Su ser interior centellea simultáneamente en la luz de las gnosis cristiana e islámica, e importa recordar que ambas escuelas espirituales encuentran muchas de sus expresiones más altas justamente en la poesía. No es por casualidad que, de todas las lenguas europeas, sea precisamente el español la lengua en la que el género de la poesía esté más vivo como expresión artística. Curiosamente, la mayoría de los poetas occidentales que han ganado el Premio Nobel de Literatura han sido hispanohablantes. Hay que decir que el género de la poesía es tan fundamental para los árabes como lo es en la cultura hispánica, y esta coincidencia nos lleva a evocar los ocho siglos de presencia cultural musulmana que España y Portugal registraron en su historia. La impronta islámica está presente aún en muchos aspectos de la cultura española siglos después que el islam fuese proscrito en la Península Ibérica. En la esfera de las artes plásticas, por ejemplo, vemos que la cerámica de origen árabe pervive como parte del arte mudéjar de España, Portugal y América Latina. Podemos observar asimismo huellas musulmanas indelebles en las artesanías y la orfebrería de Granada, Córdoba y Toledo, con sus diseños geométricos de oro sobre acero.

Introduction

It can hardly be a coincidence that the title of this collection of poems by eminent scholar Luce López-Baralt is called *Light upon Light*, as the title reflects the author's own luminous name: *Luce*. The soul of this expert in the reading and interpretation of texts, dedicated to both Sufi poetry in Arabic and Spanish mystical poetry, was illuminated at an early age by the light of Christian spirituality and, later, by the light of the esoteric teachings of Sufism. *Light upon Light* is the translation of a line from the Qu'ran, part of the famous Verse of Light in surah 24, which begins "Allah is the Light of the heavens and the earth." The phrase "light upon light" has numerous levels of interpretation, and it might be said that in a way it applies to Luce's own soul. Her inner being flickers with the light of both Christian and Islamic gnosis, and we should remember that both these spiritual schools find many of their highest expressions in poetry. Nor is it a coincidence that of all the European languages, it is Spanish in which the genre of poetry is most alive as an artistic expression. Curiously, the greatest number of Western poets who have won the Nobel Prize for Literature have written in Spanish. And one must note that poetry is as fundamental for Arabs as it is in Spanish-language culture, and this fact leads us to recall the eight centuries of Muslim cultural presence in Spain and Portugal. All these centuries after the practice of Islam was proscribed on the Iberian Peninsula, the mark left by Islam is still present in many aspects of Spanish culture. In the sphere of the plastic arts, for example, we see that the ceramics of Arab origin, especially tilework, survive as part of the Mudejar art of Spain, Portugal, and Latin America. We can also observe indelible Muslim traces in the artisanry and gold- and silver-working in Granada, Córdoba, and Toledo, with their geometric designs of gold on steel.

La misma circunstancia puede aplicarse a buena parte de la literatura española y, en especial, a la poesía mística en lengua española. Tanto santa Teresa de Ávila y san Juan de la Cruz como los escritores contemporáneos Ernesto Cardenal, Federico García Lorca, Jorge Luis Borges, Juan Goytisolo y Clara Janés han tenido acceso, de una manera u otra, a símbolos y motivos temáticos de origen sufí. El lenguaje místico del sufismo está vivo en la lengua española, circunstancia que no se da en ninguna otra lengua europea. Luce López-Baralt pertenece de lleno a este universo literario en el que la literatura española y árabe e incluso la persa confluyen —en especial, en el caso de la poesía— y se unifican en un mundo integrado de lenguaje y de sentido.

Se impone decir unas palabras sobre la autora de *Luz sobre Luz*. La conocí por primera vez hace cerca de cuarenta años en Teherán y he podido atestiguar de cerca cómo aquella joven académica se convirtió en una de las especialistas más eminentes en el campo de la literatura comparada. Luce López-Baralt ha dedicado muchos años al estudio de la literatura árabe y persa, así como a la tradición literaria hispánica, especialmente en los motivos temáticos y el lenguaje místico que ambas espiritualidades comparten. Nuestra autora está tan familiarizada con Hallach, Abu 'l-Husayn al Nuri, Ibn al-Farid e Ibn 'Arabi como lo está con santa Teresa y san Juan de la Cruz. Sus estudios acerca de la influencia de la literatura sufí sobre algunas figuras cimeras de la literatura española son fundamentales, tanto es así que le ha valido que el mundo académico la reconozca como la primera sucesora auténtica del gran islamólogo Miguel Asín Palacios.

Los estudios de Luce López-Baralt no se deben tan solo a su dominio de las lenguas más diversas y a su sólida erudición académica, sino que surgen a su vez de una profunda empatía con su campo de estudio. Esta empatía nace directamente del resplandor de la luz de la Divina Gracia sobre su alma. Sus estudios combinan, pues, el análisis lingüístico e histórico riguroso con intuiciones espirituales muy hondas, a las que la estudiosa ha podido acceder gracias a sus propias experiencias espirituales interiores. Sus poemas revelan precisamente estas experiencias.

This same tradition can be seen in a good part of Spanish literature, especially Spanish mystical poetry. Both Santa Teresa de Ávila and San Juan de la Cruz, as well as contemporary authors such as Ernesto Cardenal, Federico García Lorca, Jorge Luis Borges, Juan Goytisolo, and Clara Janés, have had access, in one way or another, to symbols and motifs of Sufi origin. The mystical language of Sufism is still alive in Spanish, unlike in any other European language. Luce López-Baralt is fully immersed in this literary universe in which the streams of Spanish and Arab — and even Persian — literature flow together, especially in the case of poetry, and meld into an integrated world of language and meaning.

I feel I must say a few words about the author of *Light upon Light*. I first met Luce almost forty years ago in Teheran, and I have been able to witness how that young academic became one of the most eminent specialists in the field of comparative literature. She has devoted many years to the study of Arab and Persian literature, as well as to the Hispanic literary tradition, especially with regard to the mystical motifs and language shared by the two spiritual traditions. Professor López-Baralt is as familiar with Hallaj, Abu l-Husayn al-Nuri, Ibn al-Farid, and Ibn 'Arabi as she is with Santa Teresa de Ávila and San Juan de la Cruz. Her studies of the influence of Sufi literature on some of the towering figures in Spanish literature are fundamental, so much so that Prof. López-Baralt has been recognized as the first true successor of the great Islamologist Miguel Asín Palacios.

Prof. López-Baralt's studies stem not just from her mastery of the most diverse languages and her solid academic erudition, but also from a profound empathy with her field of study. This empathy is born directly out of the splendor of the light of Divine Grace on her soul. Her studies combine, then, rigorous linguistic and historical analysis with deep spiritual intuitions, which she has been able to access by virtue of her own inner spiritual experiences. Her poems reveal precisely these experiences.

It is interesting to note that in the West there are very few philosophers and scholars of great stature who have in turn been poets. The

Es interesante advertir que en Occidente hay muy pocos filósofos y estudiosos de nota que a su vez hayan sido poetas. La situación es muy distinta en el islam, donde abundan los pensadores especulativos, los eruditos y sobre todo los sufíes que también se distinguen como poetas. Algunos de ellos, como poetas de primer orden. Basta recordar los nombres insignes de Ibn Sinā, Nāṣir-i Jusraw, Jayyām, Afḍāl al-Din Kāshāni, Mir Dāmād, Mullā Ṣadrā y Sabziwārī. Entre los sufíes que también fueron estudiosos, filósofos y teólogos místicos, podemos mencionar a Sanāʾi, ʿAṭṭār, Rūmī y Ŷāmī en lengua persa; y a Hallāŷ, Ibn al-Fārid e Ibn ʿArabi en lengua árabe. En cierto sentido, al ser tanto una erudita como una poeta auténtica, Luce López-Baralt pertenece más a esta tradición islámica que a la suya propia occidental. Esto no es óbice, eso sí, para que también pertenezca de lleno a la tradición cristiana, en especial al misticismo en lengua española. Los poemas reunidos en esta colección revelan claramente esta verdad. Cuando los leemos, parecería que escuchamos la música de la guitarra y el canto flamenco clásico, un arte musical representativo de la cultura española, pero que a la vez revela, misteriosamente, la presencia soterrada de un universo espiritual islámico.

Como se sabe, en distintas épocas y culturas la poesía ha servido para expresar ideas políticas o preocupaciones sociales: todos recordaremos a poetas laureados que escriben panegíricos en honor a figuras o a eventos históricos célebres. Pero la auténtica poesía mística no pertenece a esta esfera artística. Constituye, en cambio, el espejo del alma del poeta en diálogo con Dios y con los seres del mundo angelical. Este tipo de poesía nunca es amañada o superficial, sino que fluye del alma del poeta que ya se ha constituido él mismo en melodía a través de su encuentro con el Espíritu, que es quien impone a sus versos una cadencia y un ritmo que lo conectan directamente con la armonía cósmica. La poesía mística siempre ha sido detonada por una experiencia espiritual directa de Dios y fluye desde los resquicios más íntimos del alma del poeta o de la poeta, muchas veces en contra de su propia voluntad y conciencia individual. Es por eso por lo que alguno de los maestros supremos de la poesía sufí como Rūmī y Shabistarī llegaron al extremo

situation is quite different in Islam, where numerous speculative thinkers, men of erudition, and especially Sufis also distinguish themselves as poets — some, as poets of the first order. Their names include Ibn Sina, Nasir-I Khusraw, Khayyam, Afdal al-Din Kashani, Mir Damad, Mulla Sadra, and Sabziwari. Among the Sufis who were also scholars, philosophers, and mystical theologians we might mention Sana'I, Arrar, Rumi, and Jami in the Persian language and Hallaj, Ibn al-Farid, and Ibn 'Arabi in Arabic. In a certain sense, Luce López-Baralt, as both scholar and true poet, belongs more to this Islamic tradition than to her own Western one. This does not prevent her, however, from also belonging fully to the Christian tradition, especially the Christianity that embraces Spanish-language mysticism. The poems collected here clearly show that reality. When we read them, we seem to be hearing the music of classic flamenco guitar and *canto*, a music representative of Spanish culture yet revelatory, mysteriously, of the veiled presence of an Islamic spiritual universe.

As we know, in many ages and cultures poetry has served to express political ideas or social concerns: we all recall poets-laureate who have written panegyrics in honor of famous historical figures or events. But authentic mystical poetry does not belong to that realm of poetry. It is, on the contrary, the mirror of the poet's soul in dialogue with God and the beings of the angelical world. This type of poetry is never calculating or superficial. Rather, it flows from the poet's soul, which has become a melody by way of its encounter with the Spirit, and that encounter lends the verses a cadence and rhythm that connects them directly with the cosmic harmony. Mystical poetry has always been triggered by a direct spiritual experience with God, and it flows from the deepest depths of the poet's soul, often against his or her own will and individual awareness. That is why some of the supreme masters of Sufi poetry, such as Rumi and Shabistari, claimed that they were not poets at all. We can infer that Jesus' famous saying, "Seek ye first the kingdom of God, and his righteousness; and all these things shall be added unto you" (Matthew 6:33), is applicable to the mystical poets: If they seek love

de reclamar que no eran poetas. Podemos interpretar que el famoso dicho de Jesús, «Buscad primero el reino de Dios y todo lo demás se os dará por añadidura», es aplicable a los poetas místicos: si buscan el Amor y la experiencia de la Proximidad Divina, el arte de la poesía les será dado por añadidura. Los poetas místicos no se convierten en poetas con el fin de experimentar el mundo del Espíritu; antes, buscan el mundo del Espíritu y en algunos casos Dios les concede el don de la poesía para que a través de sus versos puedan revelar a los demás algo de la Verdad y de la Belleza de ese mundo espiritual que han hollado, guiándolos así al Reino Superno.

Los poemas de Luce López-Baralt pertenecen a esta categoría. Desde su juventud, esta poeta ha mantenido una conversación con Dios y con los ángeles en las dimensiones más recónditas de su alma, allá en lo más insondable de su corazón profundo. Al ser una estudiosa destacada tanto de la poesía mística española como de la islámica, ha estado, por más, dialogando en esta misma dimensión espiritual secreta con algunos de los más grandes poetas místicos de ambas tradiciones. Muchos de los poemas de esta colección constituyen, pues, un diálogo entre ella y esos grandes maestros del pasado, que son, importa destacarlo, voces espirituales vivas.

Los poemas de Luce López-Baralt que leeremos a continuación conllevan un mensaje espiritual profundo. Nos hablan del Amor y de la Sabiduría Divina a través de símbolos, alegorías y alusiones tomadas de las grandes tradiciones de la poesía islámica y occidental. La autora ha escrito poemas que pertenecen en un sentido cabal a ambos mundos culturales. Esta hazaña, tan extraña en nuestros días, le ha sido posible a Luce no solo porque se trata de una poeta sensible e inspirada, consagrada de manera personal al misticismo auténtico, sino porque es una estudiosa formidable tanto de la tradición literaria española como de la islámica. Su trabajo, en especial su poesía, constituye, por lo tanto, un puente importante entre el mundo musulmán y Occidente, puente que resulta aún más valioso en este momento histórico en el que existe tanta discordia y desavenencia, por no decir animosidad, entre ambos mundos. Celebro que después de tantos años Luce haya permitido al

and the experience of the Divine Nearness, the art of poetry will be "added unto them." Mystical poets do not become poets in order to experience the world of the Spirit; they first seek the world of the Spirit, and in some cases God grants them the gift of poetry, so that through their verses they may reveal to others something of the Truth and Beauty of that spiritual world they have trod and thereby lead those readers to the Holy Kingdom.

The poems of Luce López-Baralt belong to that category. Since she was a young woman, this poet has maintained a conversation with God and the angels in the furthest depths of her heart. As a distinguished scholar of both Spanish and Islamic mystical poetry she has also been in a dialogue in that same secret spiritual dimension with some of the greatest mystical poets of both traditions. Many of the poems in this collection are, then, a dialogue between López-Baralt and those great masters of the past, who are, one must insist, living spiritual voices.

The poems of Luce López-Baralt that we will read below convey a profound spiritual message. They speak to us of Love and Divine Wisdom through symbols, allegories, and allusions taken from the great traditions of Islamic and Western poetry. The author has written poems that belong in the truest sense to both cultural worlds. That accomplishment, so uncommon in our day, has been possible not simply because Luce is a sensitive and inspired poet, consecrated in the most personal way to authentic mysticism, but also because she is a formidable scholar of both those traditions. Her work, especially her poetry, is, therefore, an important bridge between the Muslim and Western worlds, a bridge that is all the more valuable at this moment in history, when there is so much discord and contention — not to say animosity — between the two worlds.

I applaud the fact that after so many years, Luce has allowed the public in general to glimpse the mirror that reflects her inner life. She is still very active in her life as a scholar, producing erudite studies of great importance, and I hope that she continues to be visited by the angels of poetic inspiration, so that she may in turn continue to write

público general vislumbrar el espejo que refleja su vida interior. La autora aún está muy activa redactando estudios eruditos de gran relevancia y confío en que también siga siendo visitada por los ángeles de la inspiración poética para que continúe escribiendo poesía. Oro por su bienestar y también por el de todos aquellos lectores que se sentirán tocados por sus versos y, con el favor de Dios, llevados por ellos a la morada perpetua del Espíritu, a salvo del estrépito y la cacofonía de este mundo bajo y transitorio.

Wa 'LLahu a'lam, y Dios es más sabio.

Marzo de 2014

Washington, D. C.

SEYYED HOSSEIN NASR

poetry. I pray for her well-being and also that of all those readers who will feel touched by her verses and, God willing, led by them to the perpetual "inner castle" of the Spirit, safe from the din and cacophony of this transitory world.

Wa 'Llah a'lam, and Allah is the most wise.

SEYYED HOSSEIN NASR

March, 2014

Washington, D.C.

Palabras preliminares

Esto creo no lo acabará de comprender
el que no lo hubiere experimentado
(San Juan de la Cruz)

El místico se debate «entre la imposibilidad de decir y la imposibilidad de no decir» y admito que en esta coyuntura de mi vida he terminado por cerrar filas con las palabras lapidarias de José Ángel Valente. Como estudiosa he acompañado a lo largo de muchos años la expresión literaria de los místicos más diversos, desde san Juan de la Cruz hasta Ernesto Cardenal, desde Abu l-Hasan al Nuri de Bagdad a Seyyed Hossein Nasr, sintiendo que de alguna manera muy secreta expresaban mis propias vivencias místicas. Conozco de primera mano la desesperación artística del místico, que se siente abrumado por la naturaleza ininteligible del éxtasis que lo avasalla, del Misterio que lo excede. El lenguaje es insuficiente, como afirmaba mi antiguo amigo Jorge Guillén, para expresar el instante en cúspide en que el ser humano percibe, en un estado alterado de conciencia y más allá de las coordenadas de la razón, de los sentidos, del lenguaje y del espacio-tiempo, la unidad participante con el Amor infinito. «Solo el que pasa por ello lo sabrá sentir, mas no decir», gemía san Juan de la Cruz en el Prólogo a la Subida del Monte Carmelo, sabiendo bien que era mejor reverenciar su experiencia con el silencio.

Pero no era solo la condición supraverbal de la vivencia fruitiva de Dios lo que detuvo por años mi pluma, sino la indefensión emocional que sentía ante la magnitud de lo acontecido.

¿Cómo encomendar a un puñado de signos verbales desvalidos un Misterio que me sobrepasa? Estos poemillas, a quienes encomiendo la tarea sobrehumana de balbucir algo de la experiencia mística, suelen ser muy breves —es casi como si se avergonzaran

Preface

> *This I believe no one will understand*
> *who has not experienced it.*
> SAN JUAN DE LA CRUZ

The mystic is torn, in the lapidary words of José Ángel Valente, "between the impossibility of saying and the impossibility of not saying," and I admit that at this moment in my life my balance-pan tilts toward the latter. As a scholar, for many years I have accompanied the literary expression of the most diverse mystics, from San Juan de la Cruz to Ernesto Cardenal, from Abu l-Hasan al Nuri of Bagdad to Seyyed Hossein Nasr, feeling in some very secret way that they expressed my own mystical experience. I know first-hand the mystics' artistic despair, for they feel overwhelmed by the unintelligible nature of the ecstasy that presses upon them, the Mystery so much greater than they. Language is insufficient, as my old friend Jorge Guillén would say, to express the instant at the peak of illumination when the human being, in an altered state of consciousness and beyond the coordinates of reason, of the senses, of language, and of space and time, experiences Oneness with Infinite Love. Speaking of the impossibility of conveying the mystical experience, San Juan de la Cruz complained that "He only who has passed through them can know them, but even he cannot explain them."[2] He knew, that is, that it was best to reverence his experience with silence.

But it was not just the supraverbal condition of the fruitive experience of God that immobilized my pen for years, but rather

---

2 San Juan de la Cruz, *The Ascent of Mount Carmel,* trans. David Lewis, London: Thomas Baker, 1922, p. 3.

de intentar celebrar una vivencia que quedó al margen de ellos—. Pese a su brevedad, cargan sobre sí tanto las tradiciones poéticas centenarias como las contemporáneas, que he saqueado sin pena para darle forma a mi propio canto.

Es imposible articular con palabras el fogonazo súbito en el que comprendí la urdimbre secreta del Amor que subyace al universo. El Amor último al cual estamos todos convocados. La experiencia abisal sencillamente detonó los versos, y con ellos cinceló un mundo verbal ajeno ya al éxtasis, pero, eso sí, hijo del éxtasis. Confío en que los versos conserven al menos algo del aroma del espacio trascendido que hollé un día. Nada espero de ellos, los sé vulnerables y frágiles, pero cuando se me forzaron, tuve que darles paso. Había llegado el momento, ciertamente atemorizante, de cantar lo vivido.

Querría advertir, por último, que la experiencia de unión con el Todo que aquí se celebra no es exclusiva de los santos medievales ni de los monjes reclusos. Es una gracia arbitraria de Dios propia de todas las épocas y de todas las persuasiones religiosas (y aun de agnósticos al margen de la fe eclesial estructurada) que Ernesto Cardenal me ayudó a asumir hace muchos años para consolar mi asombro: «... las experiencias místicas las pueden tener aun los que no son santos. Son caprichos de Dios, y las da a quien quiere, no porque se merezcan. Hay quienes piensan que puede darlas a los más débiles para ayudarles, porque personas más fuertes no las necesitan» (carta desde Managua, 1984). Andando el tiempo, el poeta reiteraría su alta lección espiritual en el *Telescopio en la noche oscura*, cuando siente que Dios le susurra:

> No te escogí porque fueras santo
> o con madera de futuro santo
> santos he tenido demasiados
> te escogí para variar.

Nadie —y yo menos que nadie— merece una gracia tan alta, pero aún recuerdo —*tutta tremante*— cómo fue probar un sorbo de cielo.

the emotional defenselessness I felt in the face of the magnitude of the experience. How was I to put down in a handful of hapless verbal signs a Mystery that far surpassed me? These little poems, which I charge with the superhuman task of stammering out some small part of the mystical experience, are generally quite brief. It is almost as though they blushed, timidly, at trying to convey an experience that lies outside their sphere. But despite their brevity, they carry the weight of both ages-old and contemporary poetic traditions, which I have looted, brazenly, in order to give shape to my own song.

It is not possible to articulate in words the sudden flash when I understood the secret warp of Love that underlies the universe — the ultimate Love to which we are all called. The unfathomable experience simply detonated the verses, and with the verses I paint a verbal world far distant from the ecstasy I experienced, yet one that is a child of that ecstasy. I trust that the verses preserve at least some of the fragrance of the transcendental space I set foot on one day. I expect nothing from them; I know they are vulnerable and fragile, but when they forced themselves on me, I had to let them out. The moment had come — however terrifying — to sing what I had lived.

I would like to say, lastly, that the experience of Oneness with the All that is celebrated here is not exclusive to medieval saints or cloistered monks and nuns. It is an arbitrary gift of God that can come in all times and all religious persuasions (and even to agnostics on the margin of or outside structured faith). Many years ago, Ernesto Cardenal helped console my wonderment: "Mystical experiences can be had even by those who are not saints. They are whims of God, and He gives them to whom He will, not because they deserve them. There are those who think they are given to the weakest of us to help them, because stronger people don't need them."[3] As time went on, Ernesto would reiterate this high

---

3 Letter from Ernesto Cardenal, Managua, 1984.

Aclarados estos extremos, vuelvo a las palabras de Valente: el místico se debate «entre la imposibilidad de decir y la imposibilidad de no decir». Y he aquí que se me hizo imposible callar.

Luce López-Baralt

spiritual lesson in the Telescope in the Dark Night, when he feels that God is whispering to him: "I did not choose you because you were a saint / or had the makings of a future saint / saints I've had too many / I chose you for a change."[4] No one — I, less than anyone — deserves such a high gift, yet I still recall — *tutta tremante* — what it was like to taste a sip of heaven.

These extremes clarified, I return to the words of Valente: the mystic is torn "between the impossibility of saying and the impossibility of not saying," and these poems are the result of the impossibility of my keeping silent.

Luce López-Baralt

---

4   Trans. AH.

Luz sobre luz

En la interior bodega de mi Amado bebí
un vino que me embriagó
desde antes de la creación de la viña
(San Juan de la Cruz / Ibn al-Farid/Juan Goytisolo)

Light upon Light

In the inner wine cellar I drank of my Beloved
a wine that inebriated me
even before the creation of the vineyard.
San Juan de la Cruz / Ibn al-Farid / Juan Goytisolo

Con al-Shushtari

Quien gusta el vino que yo bebí
aunque no tenga palabras

    se debe al canto.

with al-Shushtari

Those who taste the wine I drank,
though lacking words,

    shall speak in song.

Con Ernesto Cardenal

Aquel día bebí un sorbo de cielo
—ya sé a lo que sabe el cielo—.

¿Cómo será cuando apure la copa llena?

with Ernesto Cardenal

That day I drank a sip of heaven
—I now know how heaven tastes.

How will it be when I quaff the full cup?

Acerqué a mis labios
un elixir de rubíes
encendido en fuego,
fermentado sin uvas
y vendimiado sin tiempo.

Bajo aquel dosel imposible
de púrpura aterciopelada
entoné un himno al silencio.

I brought to my lips
an elixir of rubies
alight with fire,
fermented without grapes,
and aged without time.

Under that impossible canopy
of purple velvet
I intoned a hymn to silence.

Te abracé abisalmente
sin brazos,
el beso fue tan hondo
que me volví beso:

te amé con Tu propio amor.

I embraced You abyssally
without arms,
the kiss so deep
that I became Kiss:

I loved You with Your own love.

El diamante irisado de mi alma
refractó hasta el último de Tus secretos:

no sé cómo he vivido para contarlo.

The iridescent diamond of my soul
refracted even Your uttermost secret —

    I do not know how I have lived to tell it.

El misterio del Amor
cuando se enciende en Luz:
me convierte en un mosaico encendido
    que flota sobre la Nada.

The mystery of Love,
when it bursts into Light,
turns me into a flaming mosaic
 afloat upon Nothingness.

La inmensa cítara de la noche
pulsa su música callada
con tenue hilo de estrella:

Tu amor me dejó
loca de melodía.

Night's immense zither
pulses with hushed music
from its delicate string of stars:

Your love has left me
mad with melody.

Logré escuchar las estrellas sonoras
de paraísos perdidos
cuando me arrebataste al sonido de los colores.

At last I heard the vibrating stars
of paradises lost
when You snatched me away to the sound of the colors.

> *¡Qué maravilla! ¡Un jardín entre llamas!*
> (Ibn ʿArabi de Murcia)

Ay, Amor,
te dije de mi huerto encendido

¿cómo decirte ahora
de mi huerto incendiado?

Ay, Amor.

> *How wondrous! A garden set amidst flames!*
> Ibn 'Arabi

Ay, Love,
I told You of my garden and its lights.

How now to tell You
of my garden ablaze?

Ay, Love.

> *Dieu d'Abraham. Dieu d'Isaac, Dieu de Jacob,*
> *non Dieu des philosophes et des savants,*
> *Certitud, Certitude, Sentiment, Joix, Paix.*
> (Blaise Pascal)

La fragancia del sol,
el águila sideral,
la rosa infinita,
el claro lirio de la aurora,
la danza de los astros,
el séptimo castillo de la luz:

la belleza Te evoca
pero no te contiene.

>   Doy fe
>   porque Te he visto.

> *Dieu d'Abraham. Dieu d'Isaac, Dieu de Jacob,*
> *non Dieu des philosophes et des savants,*
> *Certitude, certitude, sentiment, joie, paix.*
> — Blaise Pascal

The fragrance of the sun,
the astral eagle,
the infinite rose,
the bright lily of the dawn,
the dance of the stars,
the seventh castle of light:

Their beauty evokes You
but does not contain You.

       I know that well,
       because I have seen You.

Plantamos un huerto en las esferas:
de los surcos encendidos brotaron
el sol y la luna

y juntos hicimos
una vendimia de estrellas.

We planted a garden in the spheres
and from the flaming rows the sun and moon
came forth.

Together,
we harvested stars.

Desaparecen el invocante
y el invocado:

    llegué a Tus brazos.

The invoker and invoked
disappeared —

    I came into Your arms.

Me vestiste de Ti mismo
para poderme amar,
pero me quedaba grande el vestido.

Entonces lo ajustaste compasivamente
a mi medida
que en un abrir y cerrar de ojos

      fue sin medida.

You clothed me in Yourself
to be able to love me,
but the clothing did not fit — it was too large.

So You tailored it, with compassion,
to my own measure,
which in the blink of an eye

        became measureless.

Era Tu perla escondida:
cuando me miraste al fin
me fundí de pudor en Tus brazos.

I was Your hidden pearl.
When You looked upon me at last
I melted, maidenly, into Your arms.

Me diluí en Tu esencia
con la mansedumbre de un astro apagado.
Si Te buscan,

    encontrarán mi huella.

Diluted into Your essence
with the meekness of an extinguished star.
If they seek You out,

>   they will find my traces.

Con Federico García Lorca

A la vera del agua
sin que nadie la viera
se cumplió mi esperanza.

with Federico García Lorca

At the water's edge,
seen by no one,
my hope was fulfilled.

Bebí de la fuente
que mana agua de estrellas
hasta que me convertí en lucero.

I drank from the fountain
the water of the stars flows from,
until I shined as bright as they.

Con Angelus Silesius

Me amaste con tal ímpetu
que retrocedieron, avasallados,
los serafines;
los querubines enmudecieron,
inútil ya su canto:

en medio de la nada
la senda llameante de nuestra mirada.

with Angelus Silesius

You loved me with such vehemence
that the seraphim,
overwhelmed, fell back;
the cherubim fell silent,
their song now of no use.

In the midst of the void,
the flaming path of our gaze.

> *Otra manera de arrobamiento hay, [...]*
> *que parece es arrebatado el espíritu con*
> *una velocidad que pone harto temor...*
> (Santa Teresa de Jesús)

> *Soy el que se detiene en la confluencia*
> *de los mares, [...] el que sacia su sed en*
> *la fuente de las fuentes.*
> (Abd al-Karim al-Yili)

¡Soy la luna llena que asciende!
Detengo la confluencia de los mares,
incendio todos los perfumes,
traspongo el Loto del Término,
descubro más allá de la aurora
el destello de las esmeraldas
y llego a la tierra verde del Misterio

en donde me aguardas.

> *There is another kind of rapture... [in which] the spirit*
> *seems to be hurried away with a violent speed.*
> *This... causes great fear.*
> Santa Teresa de Ávila

> *I am he who stops at the confluence*
> *of the seas, ... he who quenches his thirst*
> *in the fountain of fountains.*
> Abd al-Karim al-Jili

I am the full moon rising!
I halt the confluence of the seas,
light all the perfumes,
transpose the Lote Tree Beyond Which None May Pass,
discover the glow of emeralds
beyond the dawn,
and arrive at the green land of the Mystery,

    where You await me.

Los horizontes quedaron libres
de soles y de ocasos,
las estrellas danzaban sin órbita,
la luna roja perdía su aureola,
se anegaban los espacios,
colapsaban las horas:

¡la hebra de mi ser
entre Tus manos infinitas!

The horizons were swept free
of suns and sunsets,
the stars danced orbitless,
the red moon lost its halo,
space was flooded,
the hours collapsed —

The thread of my being
in Your infinite hands!

Iba nocturna por las islas umbrías
y, repente,

    LA LUZ

y el infinito reino del día.

I was traveling at night through the shadowy islands
when, suddenly,

    LIGHT

and the infinite realm of day.

Entro en la alfaguara plateada.
El cristal de su azogue vivo
es luz de estrella increada.

Anegada en el círculo centelleante
accedo al vértigo
y a la oblación gozosa:

yo misma soy la alfaguara.

I slip into the silvery spring.
The glass of its living mercury
is the light of an uncreated star.

Immersed in the gleaming circle,
I yield to the vertigo
and the joyous oblation —

I myself am now the spring.

Al hacerme tuya
me inscribiste en tu delicada geometría de luz,
cincelaste estrellas con diamantes,
alternaste las perlas con la espuma,
el nácar con el rocío,
la escarcha con los jazmines
hasta que resplandecí
como el sol
refractado en los mil cristales
de un mar en calma,
o como la luna
cuando arranca luceros
a un campo nevado.

Heme aquí,
tu gozosa taracea de luz:

      Tu espejo.

When I became yours
you inscribed me within your delicate geometry of light,
you chiseled stars with diamonds,
you alternated pearls with froth,
nacre with dew,
frost with jasmines,
until I blazed in splendor
like the sun
refracted in the thousand crystals
of a sea at calm,
or like the moon
when it strikes sparks
from a snow-covered field.

Behold me here:
Your joyous inlay of light —

       Your mirror.

Aspiré a ser Tu espejo
pero me convertiste
        en Tu propio rostro.

I aspired to be Your mirror
but You transformed me
　　　　into Your own face.

Con Moshé de León

Soy un palacio sin tiempo
mis cúpulas de cristal sobrepasan el cenit,
el Oriente confluye con el Occidente
en las moradas infinitas de mi medina de luz.
Mi palacio no tiene forma ni imagen:

solo lo habitas Tú.

with Moshé de León

I am a palace outside time.
My crystal cupolas rise higher than the zenith.
East joins West
in the infinite chambers of my medina of light.
My palace has neither form nor image —

You alone dwell here.

Con Clara Janés
y Vicente Aleixandre

Colapsan los hexágonos,
los triángulos y los tréboles,
los jazmines y los émbolos,
los números transfinitos,
los milenios y las eras

    mientras Tu beso se prolonga
        como el choque imposible de las estrellas.

with Clara Janés
and Vicente Aleixandre

The hexagons, the triangles, and the trefoils
collapse,
the jasmines and the emboli,
the transfinite numbers,
the millennia and the eras — all,

    while Your kiss lingers
        like the impossible clash of the stars.

Tú

Más lejos que Aldebarán
y más cerca que mi vena yugular.

You

more distant than Aldebaran
yet nearer than my jugular vein.

Con fray Luis de León

Luz no usada
aire sereno
y música extremada.

with Fray Luis de León

Light so strange
air serene
and music taken to an extreme.

Con san Juan de la Cruz

Y la caballería
a vista de las aguas
······················a
···················i
················d
·············n
···········e
·········c
·······s
····a

with San Juan de la Cruz

And the cavalry,
at the sight of the water

                              d
                        e
                    d
                n
              e
            c
          s
        a

    volaba
  que
Creía
hasta que comprendí
 que
  me
    abismaba

      was flying
    that I
I thought
until I realized that
   I was
     plunging
       into the abyss

Recibí
la Alta Noticia
como si viniera de muy lejos:

enseguida supe
que nacía de mi propio centro

I received
the Lofty News
as though it came from far, far away,

but then at once I realized
that it emerged from the center of my being.

Yissaqeni minnesiqot pihu qi tobim dodeja miyyain
[*Béseme de besos de su boca*]
(Cantar de los cantares 1,2)

bésame

abrévame
embébeme
riégame
inúndame
ahógame
encúbreme
cólmame
abrúmame
sofócame
reprímeme
suprímeme
apágame

¡bésame!

> *Yissaqeni minnesiqot pihu qi tobim dodeja miyyain*
> *[Let him kiss me with the kisses of his mouth]*
> SONG OF SONGS 1:2

kiss me

lead me to the water
let me drink my fill
irrigate me
drown me
smother me
conceal me
fill me
overwhelm me
suffocate me
repress me
suppress me
extinguish me

kiss me!

Qué bien sé yo
de ese vuelo imposible
hacia el orbe rutilante
de la Nada:
incendio de Luz viva
relámpago umbrío,
danza infinita de los astros,
danza infinitesimal de los átomos
implacable,
impasible,
imposible,

   indecible.

How fully I know
about that impossible flight
toward the sparkling orb
of Nothingness:
conflagration of living Light
dark lightning
the stars' infinite dance
the atoms' infinitesimal dance
implacable,
impassive,
impossible,

ineffable.

Aunque es de noche

qué hermoso encenderme
en la Luz negra,
en el Mediodía oscuro,
en el Rayo de tiniebla,

aunque es de noche.

Although it is night,

how lovely it is to be ignited
in the black Light
in the dark Noon,
in the Lightning-Bolt of darkness,

although it is night.

> *... esa selva virgen tan hermosa:*
> *la imposibilidad del distinguirse.*
> (Pedro Salinas)

De súbito
quedé libre del numeral tormento,
cesó la herejía de la separación
y se extinguieron los pronombres:

ya nunca más podré enunciar el Tú

> *. . . that virgin jungle so lovely:*
> *the impossibility of distinguishing ourselves.*
> PEDRO SALINAS

      Suddenly
I was freed from the numeral torment;
the heresy of separation ceased
and the pronouns were extinguished —

I will never again be able to say "You."

Dentro de este mísero cuerpo de arcilla
giran todas las esferas del universo.

Within this meager body of clay
revolve all the spheres of the universe.

Lo que supe

Es más sencillo estar al margen del tiempo
 que estar inmerso en el tiempo;

más sencillo no respirar
 que respirar;

más sencillo saberlo todo
 que no saber;

más sencillo ser el Amor
 que simplemente amar.

What I Learned

It is simpler to be on the margins of time
        than to be immersed in time,

simpler not to breathe
        than to breathe,

simpler to know everything
        than not to know,

simpler to be Love
        than simply to love.

Me sumerjo en un mar blanco sin orillas
vuelan las clepsidras y los relojes,
las horas inútiles colapsan
(eran una ficción sin sentido
que agradezco olvidar)
estoy curada del rigor de las horas:
el río de Heráclito se apaga.

Anegada en el mar blanco sin orillas
accedo a una extraña certeza:
la eternidad es sencilla.

I float in a white, shoreless sea
hourglasses and clocks blow away
hours, useless, collapse
(they were a senseless fiction
I am grateful for forgetting)
I am cured of the hours' strict time —
Heraclitus' river has halted.

Immersed in the white, shoreless sea
I yield myself to a strange assurance:
eternity is simple.

Domine non sum digna

Una palabra tuya bastará para sanarme

en una fiesta de relámpagos
comprendí al fin el alcance de la plegaria
tantas veces repetida:

>me sanaste del espacio que ocupo,
del tiempo que me transcurre,
del subconsciente que sobrellevo,
de mi cuerpo falaz.

Una palabra tuya bastó para sanarme

Domine non sum digna

>*One word of Yours will suffice to cure me*

In a fiesta of lightning bolts
I understood at last the scope of the prayer
so many times repeated:

>You cured me of the space I occupy,
>of the time that passes in me,
>of the subconscious I endure,
>of my false body.

>*One word of Yours sufficed to cure me*

Salgo a la noche,
temo al abismo,
pero la Noche
está azucarada de luces.

I go out into the night.
I fear the abyss,
but the Night
is sugared with lights.

La fuente era un cielo nocturno
de agua quemada
arrojé mis ojos sobre las aguas
vi Tus ojos
y quedó una sola
mirada encendida
flotando sobre las ondas.

The fountain was a night sky
of burned water
I cast my eyes over the waters
I saw Your eyes
and all that remained was
a single burning gaze
floating on the waves

```
            mirada sola
una                    flota
                              en el
            vacío     misma
y                      sí
      se          a
            mira
```

```
          single gaze
A                       floats
                               in the
         emptiness

     and         at itself
          gazes
```

El pájaro del día
me borra en la hora blanca,
el azogue de plata
no se atreve a reflejarme:

    soy Tuya.

The bird of day
erases me at the white hour,
the quicksilver mirror
dares not reflect me —

    I am Yours.

La Rosa era invisible

    pero su perfume la traicionó.

The Rose was invisible

    but its perfume betrayed it.

Salí de Tu mar en calma
y heme aquí
convertida en un río de asombro.

I came out of Your calm sea
and behold me here
turned into a river of wonderment.

Como la flor de loto
que surge victoriosa de la ciénaga
ascendí sobre mí misma

    y todos mis pétalos de cristal
    florecieron en Ti.

Like the lotus-flower
Rising victorious from the swamp,
I ascended above myself

        and all my crystal petals
        flowered in You.

Niels Bohr proclama la pluralidad de los mundos
y el enigma de los universos paralelos

    solo sé que soy Tuya
    en cada uno de ellos.

Niels Bohr proclaims the multiplicity of worlds
and the enigma of parallel universes.

    All I know is that I am Yours
    in every one of them.

Cultivo un huerto de estrellas:
¡Si vieran cómo brilla bajo la luna!

I tend a garden of stars.
Its fiery sparkle in the moonlight, what a sight!

Me engalanaste con luceros
y me vestiste una túnica de espejos

(querías verte).

You bedecked me with bright stars
and clad me in a tunic of mirrors.

(You wanted to see Yourself.)

Camino sin pasos hacia Ti
 y por eso no dejo huellas.

I walk toward You without walking,
    which is why I leave no footprints.

Penetré en la luz blanca
más allá del pabellón de lo invisible
y comprendí al fin el misterio
del árbol y de los cuatro pájaros.

I penetrated the white light
beyond the pavilion of the invisible
and understood at last the mystery
of the tree and the four birds.

Me elevo de sombra en sombra
mientras más perfecta es su redonda oscuridad
más me acerco al Tesoro de las Luces.

I rise from shadow to shadow.
The more perfect their round darkness,
the nearer I come to the Treasure of the Lights.

Mi Rosa inmarcesible,
¡soy tu ruiseñor rendido!

My unfading Rose,
I, your nightingale,
surrender myself to You.

En la ráfaga verde
mis gritos se hicieron nardos:
aunque no me lo digas
sé que me escuchas.

In the green gust of wind
my cries became white, fragrant flowers.
Though You do not tell me,
I know that You hear me.

La luz de la luna penetra sigilosa en el estanque
   y se cuida de no dejar su huella sobre el agua:

   Tú no te cuidaste.

Stealthily, the light of the moon enters the pool,
>taking care not to leave its footprint on the water.

>You were not so careful.

Con Abu-l-Hasan al Nuri

Entrando a los castillos interiores

Yo he sido huésped de esos clarísimos alcázares:
he hollado sus pavimentos de cristal,
supe bien del centelleo
de sus cúpulas de plata,
de la iridiscencia infinita
de sus almenas de fuego.

Cuando me anegué gozosa
en el abismo insondable de sus fosos de luz
celebré al fin la alquimia misericordiosa
de cuando el dos finalmente es Uno,
las extrañas nupcias
de cuando el dos ya no es más.

with Abu-l-Hasan al Nuri

Entering the Interior Castles

I have been a guest in those dazzling alcazars.
I have trod their crystal pavements,
I have known the gleam
of their silver cupolas,
the infinite iridescence
of their battlements of fire.

When I drowned, rapturous,
in the unfathomable abyss of their moats of light
I could celebrate, at last, the merciful alchemy
of the time when the two are finally One,
the strange nuptials
when the two are no more.

Con santa Teresa de Jesús

¡Cómo ardía la luz
en lo interior del sexto castillo!

pero lo que ocurrió en el séptimo
no es para ser contado.

with Santa Teresa de Ávila

How the light blazed
in the interior of the sixth castle!

But what happened in the seventh
is not to be told.

Eggidio di Assisi confesó:
«Vi a Dios tan de cerca que perdí la fe».
¡Cuánta razón llevaba!
En el mismo dislate

    una vez me incendié.

Giles of Assisi's confession:
"My vision of God was so clear that I lost all faith."
How right he was!
In the same folly

    I was once set afire.

Más allá de Shabistari

Noche luminosa
mediodía oscuro

Se enciende el bosque bajo la luna
un pájaro nevado atraviesa el mar
Machnún abraza a Layla entre las dunas

Noche luminosa
mediodía oscuro

Beyond Shabistari

Luminous night
darkness at noon

The forest blazes under the moon
A snow-covered bird crosses the sea
Machnun embraces Layla among the dunes

Luminous night
darkness at noon

Con Annemarie Schimmel

Los ruiseñores bajo la nieve

Los copos blancos
urdían extrañas mandalas,

la aurora boreal
parpadeaba su cielo inventado,

los témpanos azules
evocaban el tormento dantesco del frío

      (pero había ruiseñores cantando bajo la nieve...)

with Annemarie Schimmel

Nightingales in the Snowfall

White snowflakes
wove strange mandalas,

the aurora borealis
scintillated in its invented sky,

blue icebergs
evoked the Dantean torment of cold,

      but there were nightingales singing in the snowfall. . .

La montaña liberada

> *Si eres Jidr, también tú puedes franquear*
> *sin dificultad la montaña del Qaf.*
> (SHIHAB AL-DIN YAHYA SUHRAWARDI)

Opté por la cima
e inicié el ascenso,
el tiempo se hizo inmemorial
hasta que accedí al prodigio:
la montaña se desvaneció.

(nunca estuvo allí)

The Mountain Freed

> *If you are Khidr, you, too, can scale*
> *the mountain Qaf without difficulty.*
> Shihab al-din Suhrawardi

I chose the peak
and began the ascent.
The time became immemorial
until I reached the Height—
The mountain disappeared.

    (It was never there.)

Segunda Epístola a los Corintios

> *Cuerpo es alma*
> *Y todo es boda*
> (JORGE GUILLÉN)

Si en el cuerpo
o fuera del cuerpo
no lo sé

ascendida
al tercer cielo
de Pablo de Tarso
me atreví a increpar
el aturdimiento del Apóstol:
si en el cuerpo
o fuera del cuerpo
tampoco yo lo sé,

       pero no importa.

The Second Epistle to the Corinthians

Body is soul
And all is wedding
JORGE GUILLÉN

Whether at home in the body
or away from it
I know not

Ascended
to the third heaven
of Paul of Tarsus,
I dared remonstrate
with the apostle's confusion:
Whether at home in the body
or away from it
I, too, know not,

      but it doesn't matter.

Nuestro lecho florido

Shiva y Shakti hacen el amor
      en un jardín de jazmines;
la Sulamita se une a su amado
      a par de los lirios;
la amada nocturna olvida su cuidado
      entre las azucenas.

Tú y yo nos amamos
sobre un lecho florido de estrellas.

Our Flower-Strewn Bed

Shiva and Shakti make love
        in a garden filled with jasmines.
The Shulamite lies with her beloved
        among the lilies;
the beloved who comes at night forgets her care
        among the tuberoses.

You and I make love
on a bed strewn with stars.

En torno a la Azora XXIV, 35

El nicho de las luces
guarda un candil encendido
en un recipiente de cristal
que contiene una luminaria:

si lo miras
te transformas en estrella.

On Surah 24: 35

The niche of lights
holds a lighted lamp
within a crystal vessel
like a shining sun:

If you look at it,
you become a star.

Intérprete de los deseos

Ibn 'Arabi decía
que las gacelas le mostraron el Sol
en la forma de estatuas de mármol.

Entonces giró con las esferas,
sirvió en un templo de monjes cristianos
y guardó un prado multicolor en la primavera.

Interpreter of Desires

Ibn 'Arabi once said
that gazelles reflected the Sun
in the form of marble statues.

Then he revolved with the spheres,
served in an abbey of Christian monks,
and guarded a many-colored pasture in the spring.

Abu l-Hasan al-Sushtari
alcanzó la ironía suprema del juego del Amor:
supo que él mismo era la tabla y la pluma
el amante y el Amado.

Abu l-Hasan al-Sushtari
attained the supreme irony of Love's game:
He realized that he himself was the tablet and the pen,
the lover and the Beloved.

Angelus Silesius entonó
un dístico extremado:
La rosa es sin por qué. Florece porque florece.

Un día florecí en la Rosa
            también sin por qué.

Angelus Silesius intoned
an extreme couplet:
The rose has no why. It blooms because it blooms.

One day I bloomed in the Rose —
    I, too, with no why.

*Con Pablo Neruda
y Francisco Matos Paoli*

Águila sideral,
Simurg de los persas,
quetzal de la nada.
Volé con todas las aves de brillante pluma
el más alto de los vuelos:
hacia mí misma.

*with Pablo Neruda
and Francisco Matos Paoli*

Astral Eagle,
Persians' Simurgh
Quetzal of the void —
With all the birds of brilliant plumage, I flew
the highest of flights:
toward myself.

Con fray Luis de León

Mi alma se anegó
en un mar de dulzura
y me convertí en un verso de agua
    que aún canta el prodigio.

with Fray Luis de León

My soul drowned
in a sea of sweetness
and I became a verse of water
    that still sings of that wonder.

En un instante habitado por albas y espejos
al fin supe quién era.

In an instant inhabited by dawns and mirrors
I realized at last who I was.

Un pájaro cantó Tu nombre:
salmodiaba las notas
de un pentagrama imposible

    hasta que se quebró de amor.

A bird sang Your name:
It psalmed the notes
of an impossible stave

        until, from love, it faltered.

El Alpha se disuelve en el Omega
cuando llego a la meta encendida:

por aquí ya no hay camino.

with San Juan de la Cruz

The Alpha dissolves in the Omega
when I arrive at the burning goal:

There is no path here.

Con Lope de Vega

Instante al blanco vivo
relámpago de Luz increada
torbellino de Luz y de alegría,
espacio que súbitamente se incendia,
sol que nunca se hunde,
mar que vuela convertido en espejo,
ciprés ebrio en danza y ventalle
así fue Tu amor:

quien lo probó lo sabe.

with Lope de Vega

A white-hot instant,
a lightning-bolt of uncreated Light,
a whirlwind of Light and joy,
a space that suddenly catches fire,
a sun that never sets,
a sea that flies, transformed into mirror,
a cypress drunk on dancing and fanning,
that was Your love:

> *He who has tasted it knows.*

Canto sin palabras

> *Muy allá de la música-poesía*
> *muy atrás de los cantos sin palabras*
> (Luis Palés Matos)

Song Without Words

Way beyond poetry-music
way behind songs without words
                    Luis Palés Matos

¿Cómo entonar en tierra extraña
los cánticos de Yahvé?

    ¿Y cómo no entonarlos?

How, in a foreign land, can I sing
the canticles of Yahweh?

      How can I not?

Todo me lo diste Tú:

incluida la angustia
de no poder cantarlo.

You told me all —

including the anguish
of not being able to sing it.

¿Cómo me las arreglo
para gritar tu nombre en silencio?

How can I manage
to cry out Your name in silence?

Aunque llorara diamantes
no podría decirlo.

Even if I wept diamonds
   I would not be able to tell it.

Nunca más habré de creer en las palabras:
cuando llegaron a Tu umbral
estallaron como vidrios rotos.

Never more shall I believe in words.
    When they came to Your threshold
    they exploded like broken glass.

La música callada

> *Heard melodies are sweet,*
> *but those unheard are sweeter*
> (John Keats)

Psalle et sile
canta y calla
Sile et psalle
calla y canta

entona el silencio
apaga el canto

sile

        psalle

psalle

        sile

Hushed Music

> *Heard melodies are sweet,*
> *but those unheard are sweeter. . . .*
> JOHN KEATS

Psalle et sile
sing and be silent
sile et psalle
be silent and sing

Intone the silence
mute the song

sile

          psalle

psalle

              sile

Mis palabras:
monedas de nieve
relámpagos umbríos
incendio de témpanos
ruiseñores de niebla

¿Por qué insisto?

My words:
coins of snow
dark lightning-bolts
icebergs on fire
nightingales of fog

Why do I keep trying?

La pluma corría veloz sobre el papel
cuando llegó Tu amor
                      se quebró para siempre.

The pen flew swiftly across the paper.
When Your love arrived,
 it faltered forever.

Calendario de piedra,
reloj de arena,
libro de las Horas,
clepsidra antigua,
cronómetro preciso:

intento inútilmente
       medir el no-tiempo.

Stone calendar,
hourglass,
Book of Hours,
antique water-clock,
precise chronometer —

futile attempts
        to measure no-time.

El círculo de tinta

La fuente de semblantes plateados
se trocó de pronto en un oscuro círculo de tinta

    y mi dicha en desdicha.

The Circle of Ink

The fountain of silvery visages
turned, suddenly, into a dark circle of ink

and my joy, into affliction.

El tintorero Hákim de Merv
autor de *La aniquilación de la rosa*
cometió una abominable herejía:
intentó anegar en tinta
el éxtasis, el vuelo y la epifanía.

with Jorge Luis Borges

Hakim, the masked dyer of Merv,
author of *The Annihilation of the Rose*,
committed an abominable heresy:
He attempted to drown Ecstasy,
the Flight, and the Epiphany in ink.

¿Cómo decirlo?

Era un orbe de luz,
pero infinito
(entonces no era un orbe).

Era un mar sin orillas,
pero nacía en mi interior
(entonces no era un mar).

Era yo misma
pero trastocada en Tu hermosura
(entonces no era yo).

¿Cómo decirlo?

How to describe it?

It was an orb of light,
but infinite.
(So it wasn't an orb.)

It was a shoreless sea,
but born inside me.
(So it wasn't a sea.)

It was I myself
but merged into Your beauty.
(So it wasn't me.)

How to describe it?

Soy tu velo

Con Annemarie Schimmel

Las cúpulas de jazmín
el ala púrpura del arcángel
la fragancia salvaje de las lilas
el atorbellinado aleteo
de los pájaros al alba:
mojo mi pluma
en un mar azul cuajado de perlas
y sigo urdiendo palabras siempre renovadas
tan solo para ocultarte.

I Am Your Veil

with Annemarie Schimmel

Jasmine cupolas
the archangel's purple wing
the savage fragrance of lilacs
the whirlwind of birds' wings
flapping at dawn —
I dip my pen
into a blue sea clotted with pearls
and go on weaving words always renewed
only to hide You.

Aunque trocara mis palabras
en cascada olorosa de estrellas

no podría cantarte.

Though my words were transformed
into a fragrant cascade of stars,

      I could not sing You.

Si tuviera lenguaje
enseñaría a cantar a los ruiseñores.

If only I had language,
I would teach the nightingales how to sing.

La fragancia se desprende
de la rosa.
Su color blanco
flota en el aire,
sus pétalos de seda
son intangibles al tacto.
La rosa no existe:

      aún la tengo en la mano.

The fragrance breaks away
from the rose.
Its white color
floats in the air,
its silken petals
invisible to the touch.
The rose does not exist —

       I still hold it in my hand.

> *El que lo sabe, no lo dice,*
> *y el que lo dice, es porque no lo sabe.*
> (Chuang-Tzé)

Chuang-Tzé sintió nostalgia de conversación
y buscó a alguien
que hubiese olvidado las palabras

   ¡Si me hubiese encontrado!

He who knows does not speak.
He who speaks does not know.
                          CHUANG TZU

Chuang Tzu yearned for conversation
so he sought someone
who had forgotten words.

    If only he'd found me!

Fuera de sí,
'Attar de Nishapur glorificó a Dios
por haberle otorgado el lenguaje de los pájaros:

fue entonces que enmudeció para siempre.

　　　　Outside himself,
Attar of Nishapur praised God
for blessing him with the language of the birds —

　　at which moment he fell silent forever.

Han ardido las palabras
y celebro con ellas
la feria de la ceniza.

Words have blazed with fire,
and with them I celebrate
the feast day of ashes.

Entréme donde no supe...
(San Juan de la Cruz)

Mi vaso fue la luna llena
y el tiempo mi dócil esclavo;
hollé el arco de todos los colores
mientras mis palabras se derretían
como los relojes blandos de Dalí:

    ahora celebro el aturdimiento.

I entered I knew not where...
St. John of the Cross

My cup was the full moon
and time, my docile slave;
I trod the rainbow of all colors
as my words melted
like Dalí's soft watches:

      now I applaud the bewilderment.

Imagino versos,
urdo símbolos,
barajo ritmos,
oigo la música secreta
de los astros:

Dios me leerá como un poema.

I imagine verses,
weave symbols,
play with rhythms,
hear the secret music
of the spheres:

God will read me like a poem.

Me enseñaste
la ciencia de los espejos,
el lenguaje de los pájaros,
el secreto de la noche solar

y el silencio.

You taught me
the science of mirrors,
the language of birds,
the secret of the solar night

and silence.

Las palabras
a las orillas de aquel lago de plata
perdían su fijeza de ícono
y con ímpetu gozoso
se desplegaban en todas las direcciones:

dejaron pues de ser palabras,
                por lo que ahora callo.

Words
— on the shores of that silver lake —
lost their iconic fixity
and with delicious impetuosity
fanned out in all directions.

At that point they stopped being words,
                       which is why I now fall silent.

La dicha de enmudecer

El lenguaje se ha desvanecido, lo sé,
pero no cambiaría esta afasia
por todos los versos del mundo.

The Joy of Falling Silent

Language has faded away, I know,
but I would not trade this aphasia
for all the verses in the world.

Silencio:

Tembló el Misterio.

Silence:

    the Mystery trembled.

Canciones en la noche

Heu! Recidere in mea compellor!
(¡Ay! ¡Tener que replegarme de
nuevo en mí mismo!)
                    (Thomas Merton)

Songs in the Night

Heu, recidere in mea compellor!
[Alas, I am forced to fall back onto
myself!]
Thomas Merton

Un pájaro hunde su grito rojo
en el silencio,
la Nada canta a maitines:

Te has ido.

A bird's red cry is drowned
        in the silence,
Nothingness sings at matins:

      You have gone.

Yo, que una vez
me fundí con el Sol

Y ahora vivo en la tierra de una luna muerta
donde Venus es gemela de la tiniebla.

I who once
was one with the Sun

And now I live on a world with a dead moon
where Venus is the twin of darkness.

Mis oscuros minutos vacíos
son orificios en el tiempo.

Cuán difícil recordar
que viví más allá de las horas…

My dark empty minutes
are openings in time.

How difficult to remember
that I once lived beyond hours...

Una vez supe
del mapa exacto de las aguas,

¿cómo cartografiar el Océano
desde esta orilla?

Once I learned
about the exact map of the waters,

how was I to chart the Ocean
standing on this shore?

Devuelta a esta orilla
perdí la memoria del fuego:
ahora me parezco a mi sombra.

Washed up again on this shore,
I have lost the memory of fire:
Now I resemble my own shadow.

Yo fui Una contigo:
ahora sé bien
que con el dos nace la pena.

I was One with You.
Now I know
That with two, grief is born.

La senda de amatista
no conduce a ninguna parte.

Y mi corazón, en el viento invernal
vuela hacia ninguna parte.

with Annemarie Schimmel

The amethyst path
leads nowhere.

And my heart, in the winter wind,
flies nowhere.

Yo tuve un ayer de ruiseñores:
oí las melodías que embriagaron a 'Attar
en las noches fragantes de Nishapur.

Ahora me uno al llanto de Filomena,
la que entristeció para siempre a Virgilio
en los oscuros campos de Roma.

I had a yesterday of nightingales:
I heard the melodies that intoxicated Attar
in the fragrant nights of Nishapur.

Now I join Philomena's weeping,
the weeping that forever saddened Virgil
in the dark fields of Rome.

La fuente parpadea en la distancia
sus gotas de plata danzan sobre las arenas
desafiando mi sed milenaria.

¿Cómo romper el espejismo de las dunas?

The fountain twinkles in the distance.
Its silvery drops dance on the sands,
baiting my ages-old thirst.

How can the dunes' mirage be broken?

Donde Tú estabas
hay un agujero negro.

Acaricio la superficie
del orbe desolado de la esfera de la nada
y mis manos se tiznan de ceniza.

Where You once were
is a black hole now.

I caress the surface
of the desolate orb, the sphere of Nothingness,
and my hands are begrimed with ashes.

Dondequiera que haya ruinas
hay esperanza de encontrar un Tesoro:
busquen en mi corazón devastado.

Where there are ruins,
there is hope of finding a Treasure:
Search, you searchers, in my devastated heart

Con Nizami

Entré en el jardín interior
de la Perla de la Esencia;
recorrí los siete pabellones
y quedé investida
del almizcle y la plata
del rubí, del oro y la turquesa,
del sándalo y la esmeralda.

Pero hube de regresar sobre mis pasos
y ahora vivo en la nostalgia del jacinto rojo.

with Nezami

I entered the interior garden
containing the Pearl of Essence;
I wandered through its seven pavilions
and was swathed
in musk and silver,
in ruby, gold, and turquoise,
in sandalwood and emerald.

But I had to retrace my steps,
and now I live in yearning for the rubedo awakening.

¿Recuerdas?

Había unicornios
en la floresta de antaño.
Nacarados y ágiles,
galopaban por la llanura de cristal
con la gracia de las estrellas fugaces.
Ascendían por el arco de la luna
buscando los levantes de la aurora,
y bajo el centelleo de sus cascos
crecían jubilosos los jazmines.

De repente, Amor mío, les sonreíste.
Y se postraron ante Ti,
fundiéndose como el rocío.

Y yo lloré,
        envidiándolos.

with Annemarie Schimmel

Remember?

In the forest long ago
there were unicorns.
Pearly, swift, nimble,
they galloped over the crystalline plain
with the grace of shooting stars.
They ascended the arc of the moon
seeking the easts of the dawn,
and under their sparkling hooves
jasmines, jubilant, sprang up.

Suddenly, my Love, You smiled at them,
and they prostrated themselves before You,
melting like the dew.

And I wept
        In envy of them.

Una vez reflejé el Sol.

Ahora sobrellevo el brillo falaz
de una estrella extinta.

Once I reflected the Sun.

Now I radiate the tinsel light
of an extinct star.

El Sol a medianoche

> *... sobre la negrura luminosa ('anwar nurani')*
> *tengo mucho que decir, pero mejor callar.*
> (Mahmud Shabistari)

> *¡Veo Luz negra!*
> (Últimas palabras de Victor Hugo antes de morir)

Sumida en el nigredo
y el Saturno del luto
temí las tinieblas de la ausencia
y solo vi ceniza en la distancia
¿Cómo pude olvidar la oscura luz
que siempre anuncia Tu proximidad?

The Sun at Midnight

> . . . *about the shining blackness ("anwar nurani")*
> *I have much to say, but it is best to be silent.*
> — MAHMUD SHABISTARI

> *I see black light.*
> — THE LAST WORDS OF VICTOR HUGO

Mired in nigredo
and the Saturn of mourning,
I feared the shadows of absence
and saw only ashes in the distance.
How could I forget that dark Light
that ever heralds Your nearness?

Dime si desde el inmortal seguro
todavía Te acuerdas de mí.

Tell me whether, in Your fortress of immortality,
You still remember me.

Un pájaro canta lo que va a venir:

   Tu regreso.

A bird sings what is to come —

    Your return.

Translator's Note

At the beginning of my career as an academic, I was what was called, in the categorizations of the time, an "Americanist." In my particular case, this meant that I had immersed myself in the literature of the nineteenth-century United States, and that, in turn, meant that I was familiar with some fascinating moments of mystical experience in the period's writers. There was the famous spermaceti-squeezing scene in Chapter 94 of Herman Melville's *Moby-Dick*, the repeated empathic (and emphatic) onenesses of Walt Whitman ("I am large; I contain multitudes"), and the Pythagorean, almost mathematical universe of Ralph Waldo Emerson and Henry David Thoreau, into which one could infinitely expand. Seeing these mystical, or at least "mystical," moments, I began reading, more as a dilettante than a scholar, some of the canonical mystics: St. John of the Cross, St. Teresa of Ávila, Thomas Merton, and others. And because this was the sixties and seventies and eighties, I was obviously aware of the claims of "mystical" experience that were coming from those experimenting with LSD, mushrooms, peyote, and the like; some of the reports of the experiences were, indeed, uncannily similar — partly in their ineffability — to the reports of what the world considered the "true" mystics of religion and the Church. And that, in turn, led me to begin reading in the literature of comparative religion, where speculations on the mystical experience were everywhere. (By "speculations" I mean something more like "discussions" than "neurological explanations.")

At this time I was also aware of a story by Jorge Luis Borges, "The Aleph," in which the narrator-character is told that there exists, under the basement stairway of an acquaintance's house, "the place where, without admixture or confusion, all the places of the world, seen from every angle, coexist": the Aleph.[5] When the narrator, "Borges," finally describes the Aleph, he says it is "a small iridescent sphere of almost un-

---

5   Jorge Luis Borges, *Collected Fictions*, trans. Andrew Hurley, New York and London: Penguin Books, 1998, p. 281.

bearable brightness... [It] was probably two or three centimeters in diameter, but universal space was contained inside it, with no diminution in size. Each thing (the glass surface of a mirror, say) was infinite things, because I could clearly see it from every point in the cosmos. I saw the populous sea, saw dawn and dusk, saw the multitudes of the Americas, ...". (283) And here Borges embarks on a Whitmanesque "mismatched catalog." One exasperated critic said that Whitman should have been an auctioneer — auctioneers are famous for their catalogs of "lots." Both Borges and Whitman seem to have used these almost overlong catalogs of disparate "things" (I know no other word for the items) to insist on the all-inclusiveness of what they saw or experienced or, in the case of Whitman, what he *was*. Because just *saying* "oneness" or "infinity" doesn't work in fiction or poetry — it's certainly not convincing — the authors want to inject specificity. But how can one be specific about Oneness, which encompasses, which *is*, all? So these catalogs, in both cases (Borges was most certainly familiar with Whitman) — word after word after word, almost *ad infinitum*, certainly containing multitudes — stand in for "words fail me." And "words fail me" is the constant complaint, and cry, of the mystics.

Yet try they will to find words, and so the mystical literature is filled with metaphors, images, tropes for the ineffable experience. Perhaps a picture (or, in this case, word-picture) is, indeed, worth a thousand (or thousand-jillion) words. The mystic approximates by analogy, and then analogy after analogy. So through all my meanderings I had become familiar with those analogies, though not in an expert way — I had never had a mystical experience, wasn't even really religious, had never really *studied* the mystical literature, but I did have what I thought of as sympathy for it. All these writers I loved seemed to have had something like the mystical experience,[6] so I had tried to find an intellectual way into it.

---

6   Borges admitted privately (not to me, but to a trusted source of mine) that he had once had a mystical experience, but when asked, he would publicly say only, "Me, a mystic? No, I'm only a mere Argentine!"

And so I was intrigued, though respectfully wary, when, all these years later, Luce López-Baralt, my colleague and friend for some fifty years, asked me if I thought I could translate her book of poems — *mystical* poems. I thought I might give it a try, but I knew I could be in over my head, not in terms of the language and images, as "mystical" language tends to be simple and the images are, as Luce herself notes, somewhat "stock" today, as the tradition has been canonized, but rather in terms of simply understanding, catching, the allusions and the underlying experience itself and capturing it in English, in *my* words.

And indeed, as I began translating, I found that while Luce's poems were apparently simple and rather straightforward, there were lurking subtexts that I felt I was not catching. After so many years of translating, one has an intuition of depths that are beyond one's own. But I forged on, knowing that Luce would help me once I had a decent draft of the poems.

There were aspects of the translation that I needed to make decisions about: Should I use a somewhat "biblicized" language, as in the mystical poetry of the Song of Songs, with "thee" and "thou" when addressing the Lover/God? For Luce's epigraphs, quotations from poets and writers of the mystical experience, should I go to existing English translations or should I translate them in a way to bring them more closely into accord with the themes or the very vocabulary of these, Luce's, poems? Should I sometimes "clarify" or "disambiguate" images or words so that the reader in English might more clearly understand the Hispanic or Arabic, Christian or Muslim, subtext or pre-text that Luce was drawing on? (Would her readers in English, that is, be familiar with the multicultural mystical tradition that so infused and always underlay her poems?) For the first of these questions, I consulted Luce and we decided to use modern language, not to archaize the poems, as they were clearly contemporary "responses" to the experience and the tradition of the experience. For the second, I decided to use existing translations when they "fit" the poem in question, but to translate for a closer approximation when the existing English translation veered a bit off course for our purposes. And for the third, I decided to be as gentle,

as subtle as possible in clarifying words or images *when it felt absolutely necessary to do so*, but otherwise to let the opacity, or difficulty, stand, as a tantalizing "mystery" in the text.

When the draft was done, and I was as satisfied as I could be with it, I sent it to Luce for comments, corrections, clarifications, criticisms. And then we spent a lovely afternoon going over the text, word by word, image by image. Her insights were, as I had expected, tremendously helpful. Sometimes she queried a usage — "burnt" water or "burned" water? — and sometimes we came to a compromise, sometimes my original choice stood, and sometimes she led me to a better one of her own suggestion. It became a collaboration in which she was clear that I would have the last word. (And thus a collaboration in which I take full responsibility for any shortcomings; readers should not think that by using "collaboration" I am claiming that Professor López-Baralt has given it her unqualified seal of approval.) I think I "went against her" only twice, negligible usage issues, basically. I am happy with the outcome, or as happy as one can be with a translation of poetry; she says (but she is kind) that she is, too.

I am honored and delighted to be able to bring these lovely poems to an English-language readership, grateful that Luce and the publisher have enabled me to transport them across the seas, as it were, to a new audience. In my experience, they should be dipped into here and there; this is not a book to be read through, poem by poem, in one or two sittings. They are, as I say, apparently simple, but they are profound and often very moving, the record of a mystic's attempt to render her experience so that others may in some way share it. Mystics have always been generous; they have tried — so hard — to make their moments of ineffable experience available to others. This volume is, in my opinion, another example of that generosity, and I, for one, accept the gift most gratefully.

Andrew Hurley

San Juan, September 2023

www.ingramcontent.com/pod-product-compliance
Lightning Source LLC
Chambersburg PA
CBHW040319170426
43197CB00022B/2962